A. K Browne

The Story of the Kearsarge and Alabama

A. K Browne

The Story of the Kearsarge and Alabama

ISBN/EAN: 9783743399167

Manufactured in Europe, USA, Canada, Australia, Japa

Cover: Foto ©ninafisch / pixelio.de

Manufactured and distributed by brebook publishing software
(www.brebook.com)

A. K Browne

The Story of the Kearsarge and Alabama

THE STORY

OF THE

KEARSARGE

AND

ALABAMA.

SAN FRANCISCO:

HENRY PAYOT & CO., PUBLISHERS.

1868.

The Author is induced to publish this narrative of the Kearsarge and Alabama, from the want that exists of a popular, detailed, and yet concise account of the engagement between the two vessels.

THE STORY.

On Sunday, June 12th, 1864, the U. S. Steamer Kearsarge was lying at anchor in the Scheldt, off Flushing, Holland. Suddenly appeared the cornet at the fore—an unexpected signal, that compelled absent officers and men to repair on board. Steam was raised, and immediately after a departure made, when all hands being called, the nature of the precipitate movement became apparent. Captain Winslow, in a brief address, announced the welcome intelligence of the reception of a telegram from his Excellency, Mr. Dayton, Minister Resident at Paris, to the effect that the notorious Alabama had arrived the day previous at Cherbourg, France; hence, the urgency of departure, the probability of an encounter, and the confident expectation of her destruction or capture. The crew responded by cheers.

The succeeding day witnessed the arrival of the Kearsarge at Dover, England, for dispatches, and the day after (Tuesday) her appearance off Cherbourg Breakwater. At anchor in the harbor was seen the celebrated Alabama—a beautiful specimen of naval architecture, eliciting encomiums for evident neatness, good order, and a well-disciplined crew, indicative of efficiency in any duty required. The surgeon of the Kearsarge proceeded on shore and obtained pratique for boats. Owing to the enforcement of the neutral twenty-four hour regulation, to anchor, became inexpedient; the result was the establishment of a vigilant watch, alternately, at each of the harbor entrances, which continued to the moment of the engagement.

On Wednesday, Captain Winslow paid an official visit to the Admiral commanding the Maritime District and the U. S. Commercial Agent, bringing on his return the unanticipated news that Captain Semmes declared his intention to fight. At first, the assertion was hardly credited, the policy of the Alabama being regarded as in opposition to a conflict, but even the doubters were speedily half convinced when the character of the so-called challenge was disclosed, viz. :

"C. S. S. Alabama, Cherbourg, June 14th, 1864.

"To A. Bonfils, Esq.,

"Cherbourg—

"*Sir:* I hear that you were informed by the U. S. Consul, that the Kearsarge was to come to this port solely for the prisoners landed by me, and that she was to depart in twenty-four hours. I desire you to say to the U. S. Consul that my intention is to fight the Kearsarge, as soon as I can make the necessary arrangements. I hope these will not detain me more than until to-morrow evening, or after the morrow morning at farthest. I beg she will not depart before I am ready to go out.

"I have the honor to be

"Very respectfully,

"Your obedient servant,

"R. SEMMES,

"Captain."

This communication was sent by Mr. Bonfils to the U. S. Commercial Agent, Mr. Liais, with a request that the latter would furnish a copy to Captain Winslow for his guidance. There was no other defiance to combat. The letter that passed between the commercial agents, was the challenge about which so much has been written. Captain Semmes indirectly informed Captain Winslow of his desire for a combat. Captain Winslow made no reply, but prepared his ship to meet the opponent, thereby tacitly acknowledging the so-called challenge and its acceptance.

Requisite preparations were immediately insti-

tuted for battle, with no relaxation of the watch. Thursday passed; Friday came, and yet no Alabama appeared. According to report, important arrangements were being effected; a zeal was displayed in the reception of coals, the transmission of valuables on shore, and the sharpening of swords, cutlasses, boarding-pikes, and battle-axes. To the observer this preparation confirmed the assurance of the certainty of a fight. An intended surprise by night was suggested, and measures precautionary taken. Dispatches were brought from Mr. Dayton, Minister at Paris, by his son, who with difficulty had obtained permission from the Admiral commanding to visit the Kearsarge. To preserve a strictly honest neutrality, the French authorities had prohibited all communication with the respective vessels. Mr. Dayton expressed the opinion that the Alabama would not fight, though acknowledging the prevalence of a contrary impression at Cherbourg; he departed for the shore with intention to proceed immediately to Paris. In taking leave of the Admiral, the latter mentioned the fixed determination of Captain Semmes to engage with the Kearsarge on the day following (Sunday), and that he imparted this intelligence, since no subsequent communication could be had with the Kearsarge. Mr. Dayton consequently deferred his departure, witnessed the action, tele-

graphed to Paris the result, and was one of the first to repair on board and offer congratulations. He passed a portion of Saturday night endeavoring to procure a boat to dispatch to the Kearsarge the information acquired, but so securely was the coast guarded by the enforcement of the Admiral's orders, that all his efforts were useless.

At a supper in Cherbourg on Saturday night, several officers of the Alabama met sympathizing French friends—the impending fight being the chief topic of conversation. In confidence of an easy victory, they boastingly proclaimed the intention either to sink the Federal or gain another corsair. They rise with promise to meet the following night to renew the festivity as victors, are escorted to the boat, and separate with cheers and wishes for a successful return.

Sunday the 19th comes; a fine day, atmosphere somewhat hazy, little sea, moderate westerly wind.

At 10 A.M. the crew are inspected at quarters and dispersed to attend divine service at 11 o'clock. Seemingly no one thought of the Alabama, for so long awaited and not appearing, speculation as to her probable advent had ceased. At 10.20 the officer of the deck reports a steamer coming from Cherbourg, a frequent occurrence, and consequently creates no excitement. Soon, by the aid of a glass, he descries the enemy, and shouts: " The

Alabama!" Instantly all hands are called and the
ship cleared for action.

The position of the Kearsarge was off the east-
ern entrance to the harbor, at a distance of nearly
three miles, the Alabama approaching from the
western entrance, escorted by the French iron-clad
frigate La Couronne, and followed by a fore-and-
aft rigged steamer, flying the English yacht flag,
the Deerhound. The frigate having convoyed the
Alabama outside the limit of French waters, with
characteristic neutrality, steamed back into port
without delay; the yacht remained in proximity to
the scene of action. To avoid a question of juris-
diction, and to prevent an escape of the Alabama
to neutral waters in the event of a retreat, the
Kearsarge steamed to sea making final preparations,
the last being the sanding of decks (sufficiently
suggestive of sober thoughts), followed by the
enemy, until a distance of about seven miles from
the shore was attained, when at 10.50 the Kearsarge
wheeled, bringing her head in shore, and presented
starboard battery, being one and a quarter miles
from her opponent: the Kearsarge advanced rapidly, and at 10.57 received the first broadside of
solid shot at a distance of eighteen hundred yards
from the Alabama. This broadside cut away a
little of the rigging, but the shot chiefly passed
over or fell short. With increased speed the

Kearsarge advanced, receiving a second and part of a third broadside with similar effect. Arrived within nine hundred yards of the Alabama, the Kearsarge, fearing a fourth broadside with evident raking results, sheered and broke her silence by opening with the starboard battery. Each vessel was now pressed under a full head of steam, each employing the starboard battery, and to obviate passing each other too speedily, and to maintain the bearing of the respective broadsides, the circular method of fighting was necessitated, each steering around a common center, from a quarter to half a mile apart.

The action was now fairly commenced. One of the shot of the first broadsides of the Kearsarge carried away the spanker-gaff of the enemy, and caused his ensign to come down by the run. This incident was received as a favorable omen by the fortunate crew, who cheered vociferously and went with increased confidence to their work. Wild and rapid was the firing of the Alabama, that of the Kearsarge being deliberate, precise, and almost from the commencement productive of death, destruction, and dismay. The Kearsarge gunners had been cautioned against firing without direct aim, advised to elevate or depress the guns with deliberation, and though subjected to an incessant storm of shot and shell, proceeded calmly to their

3

duty, and faithfully complied with the instructions. The effect upon the enemy was readily perceived; nothing restrained the enthusiasm of the crew. Cheer succeeded cheer, caps thrown in the air or overboard, jackets discarded, one encouraging the other, sanguine of victory, shouting as each projectile took effect: " That is a good one;" "that told;" "give her another;" " down boys;" " give her another like the last;" and so on, cheering, exulting, joyous to the end. After exposure to an uninterrupted cannonading for eighteen minutes without casualties, a sixty-eight-pound Blakely shell passed through the starboard bulwarks below main rigging, exploded upon the quarter-deck, and wounded three of the crew of the after-pivot gun. With these exceptions, not an officer or a man of the Kearsarge received the slightest injury. The unfortunates were speedily taken below, and so quietly was the action performed, that at the termination of the fight a large portion of the crew were unaware that any of their comrades were wounded. Two shot entered the ports occupied by the thirty-twos, where several men were stationed, and yet none were hit. A shell exploded in the hammock-netting and set the ship on fire; the alarm calling to fire-quarters was sounded, and persons specially detailed for a like emergency, promptly extinguished the flames, while the re-

mainder of the crew continued at the guns without interruption.

Terrific was the effect of the eleven-inch shell upon the crew of the doomed ship: many were torn asunder by shell direct, or horribly mutilated by splinters. Her decks were covered with blood and the debris of bodies. One gun (after-pivot) had its crew renewed four times, fourteen out of nineteen men being disabled during the action. The carnage around this gun was more frightful than elsewhere; so great was the accumulation of blood and fragments of limbs, that a removal was required before the gun could be worked. A man upon the bowsprit is struck in the abdomen by a shot, staggers aft holding up his entrails, and near the main hatch falls dead. Another is cut in twain, one-half of the body going down the engine hatch, the other half remaining on deck. A poor wretch paralyzed by fear leaves his station and vainly seeks safety by a plea of indisposition; he is ordered to resume his position at the gun, and not obeying, is killed by a pistol shot from the officer commanding the division.

It is truly wonderful that so few casualties should have occurred on board the Kearsarge with so large a percentage to her adversary—the first having fired one hundred and seventy-three shot and shell, and the second nearly double that num-

ber. Probably no future similar combat will occasion like results.

The fight continues. The eleven-inch shell tell with astonishing precision; one penetrates a coal bunker, and immediately a dense cloud of coal-dust rises and like a pall hovers over the fated ship. Others strike near the water-line between the main and mizzen masts, explode within board, or passing through burst afar off. Crippled and torn the Alabama moves less quickly and begins to settle by the stern, yet relaxes not her fire, but returns successive broadsides, ever without disastrous effect. Captain Semmes witnesses the dreadful havoc made by the shell, especially by those of the after-pivot gun, and offers a reward for its silence. Soon his battery is turned upon the particular offending gun with endeavor to compel its abandonment; in vain, for its work of destruction goes on. Captain Semmes places sharpshooters in the quarter boats to pick off the officers; in vain, for none are injured. He views the surrounding devastation—a sinking ship, rudder and propeller disabled, a large portion of the crew killed or wounded, while his adversary is apparently but slightly damaged. He has completed the seventh rotation on the circular tract and is conscious of defeat. He seeks to escape by setting all available sail (foretrysail and two jibs), leaves

the circle and heads for the neutral waters of the French coast. The speed of his vessel is lessened; in winding she presents the port battery with only two guns bearing, and exhibits gaping sides. The Alabama is at the mercy of the Kearsarge. Captain Semmes calls his officers aft, briefly states the condition of the two vessels, and orders a surrender to prevent a further loss of life.

The colors are struck and the Kearsarge ceases firing. Two of the junior officers of the Alabama swear they will never surrender to a "damned Yankee," but rather go down in the ship; in a mutinous spirit they rush to the two port guns and open fire upon the Kearsarge. Captain Winslow, amazed at this unwonted conduct of an enemy who had hauled down his flag in token of surrender, exclaimed: "He is playing us a trick, give him another broadside." Again the shot and shell go crashing through the bulwarks, carrying death and destruction; the Kearsarge is laid across the bows for raking and in position to employ grape and canister with deadly effect. Over the stern of the Alabama is displayed a white flag, her ensign half-masted, union down; Captain Winslow for the second time orders a cessation of firing.

Captain Semmes in his report says: "Although we were now but four hundred yards from each other, the enemy fired upon me five times after my

4

colors had been struck. It is charitable to suppose that a ship-of-war of a christian nation could not have done this intentionally." He had not the generosity to afford the explanation; he is silent as to the renewal of the fight after his surrender; an act which in christian warfare would, in severe justice, have authorized the Kearsarge to continue firing until the Alabama had disappeared beneath the waters; nay, even to have refused quarter to the survivors.

Thus ended the fight after a duration of one hour and two minutes.

Boats were now lowered from the humbled Alabama. A master's mate, an Englishman, Fullam by name, came alongside the Kearsarge with a few of the wounded, reported the disabled and sinking condition of his vessel, and asked for assistance.

Captain Winslow demanded: " Does Captain Semmes surrender his ship?" "Yes," was the reply. Fullam then solicited permission to return to the Alabama with his boat and crew to assist in rescuing the drowning, pledging his word of honor that when this act was accomplished, he would come on board and surrender himself a prisoner. Unhappily Captain Winslow granted the request. With less generosity, he could have detained the rebel officer and men, supplied their places in the

boat from his own ship's company, secured more prisoners, and afforded equal aid to the distressed. The generosity was abused as the sequel shows. Fullam pulled to the midst of the drowning, rescued several officers, proceeded to the Deerhound, cast his boat adrift, and basely violated his proffered word of honor.

The Deerhound, after the conclusion of the fight, appears upon the scene, and plays an important part. This yacht was built by the Messrs. Laird, at the same yard with the Alabama. Coming under the stern from the windward, the Deerhound was hailed, and her commander requested by Captain Winslow to run down to the Alabama and assist in picking up the men of the sinking vessel. Or, as Mr. Lancaster reported: "The fact is, that when we passed the Kearsarge the captain cried out,—'For God's sake do what you can to save them;' and that was my warrant for interfering in any way for the aid and succor of his enemies." The Deerhound steamed towards the Alabama, which sank almost immediately after, lowered her boats, rescued Captain Semmes, thirteen officers, and twenty-six men, leaving the rest of the survivors to the boats of the Kearsarge, and departed directly for Southampton. Captain Winslow permitted the yacht to secure his prisoners, anticipating their subsequent surrender. Again was his

confidence in the integrity of a neutral misplaced. The assistance of the yacht, it is presumed, was solicited in a spirit of chivalry, for the Kearsarge comparatively uninjured, with but three wounded, possessed of a full head of steam, was in condition to engage a second enemy: instead of remaining at a distance of about four hundred yards from the Alabama, and from this position sending two boats (others being unserviceable), the Kearsarge by steaming close to the settling ship and in midst of the vanquished, could have captured all—Semmes, officers, and men.

The Deerhound steams rapidly away. An officer approaches Captain Winslow and reports the presence of Captain Semmes and many officers on board the English yacht, considering the information authentic as it was obtained from certain prisoners; he suggests the propriety of firing a shot to bring her to, and asks permission. Captain Winslow chivalrously replies in the negative, declaring that no Englishman who flies the royal yacht flag, would act so dishonorable a part as to run away with his prisoners when he had been asked to save them from drowning. Meanwhile the Deerhound increases the distance from the Kearsarge; another officer addresses Captain Winslow in language of similar effect, but with more positiveness, that Semmes and his officers were on

board the yacht endeavoring to escape. With un-
diminished confidence in the honor of the English
gentleman, with continued chivalric spirit Captain
Winslow refuses to have a shot fired, not credit-
ing the flight, saying that the yacht was "simply
coming round," and would not go away without
communicating. "I could not believe that the
commander of that vessel could be guilty of so
disgraceful an act as taking our prisoners, and
therefore took no means to prevent it." Without
this trust in chivalry, Captain Winslow might have
arrested the yacht in her flight, if only as a pru-
dential motive, reserving final action as to the
seizure of the passengers when time had been
afforded for reflection.

No shot is fired: the Deerhound finally dis-
appears with the great prize, Semmes, and thus
passed an opportunity of making this brilliant engagement one of the most complete and satis-
factory in naval history.

Captain Winslow erroneously thought that the
Deerhound would not run away with the rescued
persons: in this opinion he was probably alone.
An excitement occurred as a consequent; an ex-
pression of regret for the escape of the yacht and
her coveted prize, after being as it were within
reach of the victors. The bitterness of the regret
was manifest. The famed Alabama, "a formid-

able ship, the terror of American commerce, well armed, well manned, well handled," was destroyed, "sent to the bottom in an hour," but her notorious commander had escaped : the eclat of victory seemed already lessened.

At 12.24 the Alabama sank in forty-five fathoms of water, at a distance of about four and a half miles from Cherbourg Breakwater, off the west entrance. She was severely hulled between the main and mizzen masts, and commenced settling by the stern before the termination of the conflict. Her crew had jumped into the sea, supporting themselves by portions of the wreck, spars, and other accessible objects, the water swept over the stern and upper deck, and when thus partially submerged, the mainmast, pierced by a shot, broke off near the head, the bow lifted from the waves, and then came the end. Suddenly assuming a perpendicular position, caused by the falling aft of the battery and stores, straight as a plumb-line, stern first, she went down, the jibboom being the last to appear above water. Down sank the terror of merchantmen, riddled through and through, and as she disappeared to her last resting place, not a cheer arose from the victors. To borrow the language of the Liverpool *Courrier :* " Down under the French waters, resting on the bed of the ocean, lies the gallant Alabama, with all her guns aboard,

and some of her brave crew, waiting until the sea yields up its dead."

Mounted on the summit of an old church tower, a photographic artist obtained a good negative of the contest. An excursion train from Paris arrived Sunday morning, bringing hundreds of pleasure-seekers who were unexpectedly favored by the spectacle of a sea-fight. The events of the day monopolized the conversation of Parisian society for more than a week.

This grand artillery duel, or Sunday gladiatorial combat, occurred in the presence of more than fifteen thousand spectators, who upon the heights of Cherbourg, the breakwater, and rigging of men-of-war, witnessed "the last of the Alabama." Among them were the captains and crews of two merchant ships burnt by the daring rover a few days before her arrival at Cherbourg. Their excitement during the combat was intense, and their expressions of joy to the victors at the result, such as only those who had suffered from the depredations of the Alabama could give utterance to. Many were desirous to go on board the Kearsarge to participate in the action, but so strictly was the neutrality law observed, no intercourse was allowed.

The Alabama's wounded were brought on board the Kearsarge for surgical attendance. Seventy persons, including five officers, were saved by

the boats. The conduct of Dr. Llewellyn, native of Wales, Assistant Surgeon of the Alabama, deserves mention. He was unremitting in attention to the wounded during the battle, and after the surrender, superintended their removal to the Kearsarge, nobly refusing to leave the ship while one remained. This humane duty performed, with inability to swim, he caused two empty shell boxes to be attached to his waist, an improvised life-preserver, and thus prepared leaped overboard. In the hurried adjustment of the shell boxes, sufficient care was not taken to maintain the center of gravity, the unfortunate gentleman failed to keep his head above water, and before aid could be derived from his struggling comrades, he was dead.

At 3.10 P.M. the Kearsarge anchored in Cherbourg harbor; the wounded were transferred the same evening to the Hopital de la Marine, and all the prisoners, officers excepted, were paroled and set on shore before sunset. The crew of both vessels harmonized after the fight, the conquerors sharing their clothes, supper, and grog with the conquered.

The total casualties of the Alabama are not known, estimated at forty-seven—a striking contrast to the three of the Kearsarge. Two of these three recovered; one, the brave Gowin, died in hospital. The behavior of this gallant sailor dur-

ing and after the battle, as described by the Executive Officer and Surgeon, is worthy of the highest commendation. Stationed at the after-pivot gun, by the explosion of a shell, he was seriously wounded in the left thigh and leg; in the agony of pain, and exhausted from the loss of blood, he dragged himself to the forward hatch, concealing the severity of injury, that his comrades might not leave their stations for his assistance: fainting, he was lowered to the care of the surgeon, whom poor Gowin, in acuteness of suffering, greeted with a smile, saying: " Doctor, I can fight no more and so come to you, but it is all right, I am satisfied, for we are whipping the Alabama;" and subsequently: " I will willingly lose my leg or my life if it is necessary." Lying upon his mattress he paid strict attention to the progress of the fight, as far as could be elicited by the sounds on deck—his face beaming with satisfaction whenever the cheers of his shipmates were heard ; with difficulty he waved his hand over his head and joined in each exulting shout with a feeble voice. At times he would comfort the other wounded by an earnest assurance that " victory is ours!" Directly after the fight he desired the surgeon to render him no further attention, for he was "doing well," requesting that all his time should be devoted to the "poor fellows of the Alabama." In

the hospital he was resigned, thankful for being the only victim, proud of his ship and shipmates, frequently asserting his willingness to die after so glorious a victory. " This man, so interesting by his courage and resignation," wrote the French surgeon-in-chief, with uniform patience and cheerfulness, enlisted general sympathy; all anxiously desired his recovery and sincerely regretted his decease. Certainly one of the most interesting events of the action is the heroic conduct of the brave Gowin.

An incident that ever occasions gratification in its relation, was the singular coincidence of the lowering of the rebel colors by an early shot from the Kearsarge, and the unfolding of the victorious flag by a shot from the last volley of the Alabama, prior to surrender. At the main peak of the Kearsarge the colors were stopped, that they might be displayed if the ensign was carried away, and to serve as the emblem of victory in case of a happy success. It will be remembered that the Alabama's colors were brought down by a shot from one of the first broadsides of the Kearsarge,—an auspicious omen for the sailor at the commencement of battle. A shot from the last broadside of the Alabama passed high over the Kearsarge, striking and carrying away the halyards of the colors at the main peak, and in so doing, pulled sufficiently

to break the stop, and thereby unfurled the triumphant flag at the moment the rebel ensign was struck in token of submission.

The Alabama was destroyed—the Kearsarge being so little damaged, that if required, could have engaged another enemy. It is surprising that the Alabama's fire should have produced so moderate an injury, for, according to report, over three hundred shot and shell were discharged; of these, thirteen took effect in the hull, and fifteen in sails, rigging, boats, and smoke-stack. Luckily, a one hundred and ten-pounder rifle shell which lodged in the stern post, raising the transom frame, and a thirty-two-pounder shell that entered forward of forward-pivot port, crushing water-ways, did not explode.

Captain Semmes, in his official report, says: " At the end of the engagement it was discovered by those of our officers who went alongside the enemy's ship with the wounded, that her midship section on both sides was thoroughly iron-coated. This planking had been ripped off in every direction by our shot and shell, the chain broken and indented in many places, and forced partly into the ship's side. The enemy was heavier than myself, both in ship, battery, and crew; but I did not know until the action was over that she was also iron-clad." The chain-plating of the Kearsarge,

the " iron-clad " of Captain Semmes, consisted of one hundred and twenty fathoms of sheet chains covering a space amid-ships of forty-nine and one-half feet in length by sixteen feet two inches in depth, stopped up and down to eyebolts with mar-lines, secured by iron-dogs and employed for the purpose of protecting the engines when the upper part of the coal bunkers was empty, as happened during the action. The chains were concealed by inch deal boards as a finish. The chain-plating was struck twice, by a thirty-two pound shot in starboard gangway, which cut the chain and bruised planking, and by a thirty-two-pounder shell, which which broke a link of the chain, exploded, and tore away a portion of the deal covering. Had the shot been from the one hundred and ten-pounder rifle, the result would have been different, though without serious damage, because the shot struck five feet above the water line, and if sent through the side would have cleared the machinery and boilers. It is proper therefore to assert that in the absence of the chain-armor the result would have remained the same, notwith-standing the common impression at the time, of an "iron clad " contending with a wooden ves-sel. The chains were attached to the ship's side more than a year previous to the fight, while at the Azores; in subsequent visits to European

ports they had attracted notice and caused repeat-
ed comment. Strange that Captain Semmes did
not know of the chain-armor before the fight;
supposed rebel spies had been on board, there was
no attempt at concealment; the same pilot was
employed by both vessels and visited each during
the preparation for battle.

One hundred and sixty-three was the number
of the crew of the Kearsarge, including officers;
that of the Alabama not definitely known, but
from the most reliable information estimated at
nearly the same. The tonnage of the former
1031, of the latter 1044. The battery of the
Kearsarge consisted of seven guns, two eleven-
inch pivots, smooth bore, one twenty-eight-pound-
er rifle, and four light thirty-two pounders; that
of the Alabama of eight guns, one sixty-eight-
pounder pivot, smooth bore, one one hundred and
ten-pounder rifle pivot, and six heavy thirty-two
pounders. Five guns were fought by the Kearsarge, seven by the Alabama, both with the starboard batteries. The Kearsarge had made thirteen
and one-half knots an hour under steam, the Alabama never exceeded thirteen, and at the time of
the action was only equal to ten. The vessels were
not unequally matched in size, speed, crew, and
armament, displaying a similarity not often witnessed in naval battles. The contest was decided

by the superiority of the eleven-inch Dahlgrens over the Blakely rifle and smooth bore, in connection with the greater coolness and accuracy in aim of the gunners of the Kearsarge.

"So ends the story of the Alabama," quoting again from the Liverpool *Courier*, "whose journal would be the most interesting volume of ocean literature; whose ubiquity scared the commerce of America from the seas; whose destructive powers have ruined property belonging to the northerns valued at upwards of three millions of money; whose actions very nearly involved these countries in war with the United States. The Americans are indignant that the ship was built by British hands, of British oak, armed with British guns, and manned by British sailors."

Numerous inaccuracies, suppressions, exaggerations, and discrepancies exist in most of the accounts of this renowned naval engagement. The first reports published in Europe were characterized by contradictions sufficient to confuse any reader. This variance was noted by the London *Daily News* in the following manner: "The sceptic who called history a matter-of-fact romance, should have lived in our day, when a naval action is fought off Cherbourg on a Sunday, and reported to the London and Paris newspapers on the Monday morning, no two reports agreeing in any single

fact, except in the result. In our enlightened epoch of incessant, instantaneous, and universal inter-communication, the difficulty of getting at the simple facts of any passing incident, in which conflicting sympathies are concerned, increases in proportion to the increasing celerity and certainty with which the materials of history are gathered. Some allowance, no doubt, may be made for eye-witnesses on shore of a naval engagement seven miles out at sea. Their 'powerful glasses' are liable to that peculiar inaccuracy of sight which distance, excitement, and smoke produce. A French gentleman, for instance, who from Cherbourg Breakwater looked on at the American duel on Sunday last, wrote a graphic letter to the *Debats*, with a postcript to the effect that he had just discovered that the account in his letter was entirely wrong."

Here ends the present story of the Kearsarge and Alabama. It is the truth told honestly.

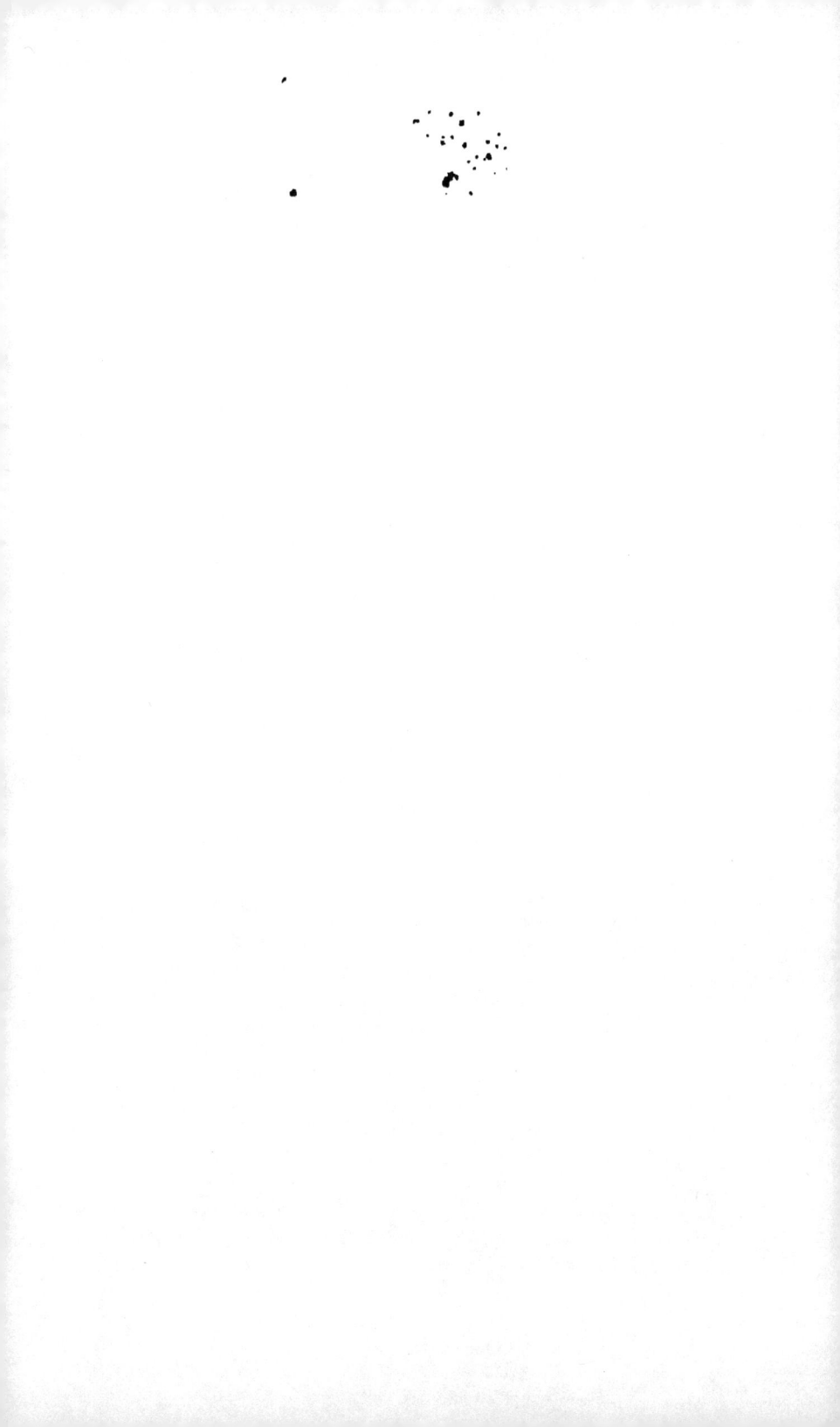

www.ingramcontent.com/pod-product-compliance
Lightning Source LLC
Chambersburg PA
CBHW022036080426
42733CB00007B/848